GOOD LORD,

WHERE ARE YOU?

Prayers for the 20th Century

Based on the Psalms

LESLIE F. BRANDT

Concordia Publishing House

St. Louis, Missouri

Concordia Publishing House, St. Louis, Missouri
Concordia Publishing House Ltd., London, E. C. 1
© 1967 Concordia Publishing House
Library of Congress Catalog Card No. 67-17974

Contents

Preface

I first read the Book of Psalms through at the age of 10. I don't remember what they said to me at that time, but in the ensuing years they often articulated my feelings and verbalized my prayers as a struggling saint. It was just recently, in the 20th year of my ministry, that I began to "rewrite" a few of them for my church bulletin. These paraphrases on the Psalms appeared to fill a need, and I was encouraged to continue and eventually to submit a collection of them for possible publication.

I have tried to express what these Psalms say to me and about me. It is just possible that they may reveal to other readers something about themselves and give them a means of expressing their actual feelings in their conversations with God. These humble offerings are by no means an attempt to be scholarly or textual. On the other hand, they ought to indicate something of the honesty and humanity of the psalm writers in their daily conflicts and to encourage us to be as honest in our pursuit of truth and our walk with God.

I have taken liberties in paraphrasing these Psalms. If these efforts serve to make them more relevant for modern saints and if they may help to express more adequately the perpetual conflicts of a child of God in our complex society, they will serve their purpose.

LESLIE F. BRANDT

Paraphrase on Psalm 1

The man who chooses to live a significant life
is not going to take his cues from the religiously
indifferent.
Nor will he conform to the crowd
Nor mouth his prejudices
Nor dote on the failures of others.

His ultimate concern is the will of God.
He makes his daily decisions in respect to such.
He can be compared to a sturdy tree planted in
rich and moist soil.
As the tree yields fruit, so his life manifests
blessing for others.
His life is productive and effective.

This is not true concerning the ungodly.
They are like sand in a desert storm
Or leaves in an autumn wind.
They cannot stand against the judgments of the
eternal God.
And they are most uncomfortable amongst those
who demonstrate genuine faith in the God of
righteousness.

The children of God walk in the course that God
has ordained.
The children of unbelief walk in paths of self-
destruction.

Paraphrase on Psalm 2

Why is it that dictators and governments throughout our world persist in persecuting the people
of God?
They may be divided in everything else,
But they unite in their endeavors to free themselves from the restraints of religion.

As disconcerting as this is to me,
Our great God laughs at their foolish efforts.
And His laughter will have the sound of fury in
that day that He determines to act against them.
He will reveal to them who truly is Lord and
King.

But to Me, even in the midst of My conster-
nation,
He speaks as a loving Father.
"You are My Son and Servant," He says.
"Trust in Me; the destiny of the world is in
Your hands.
You shall be the Overcomer;
You shall frustrate their attempts to destroy
You."

So wise up, you who sit in high places.
Begin serving the God you are trying to silence.
Bow your hearts in submission before He crowns
your heads with divine wrath.

Only those who rest in God's will are really
secure.

Paraphrase on Psalm 4

Dear God, respond to Your servant in distress;
Make room in Your loving grace for a disciple in
   despair;
Listen to the agonizing cries of a child who is
   depressed and unhappy.

   O you people around me, you who I thought
      were my friends,
   Why do you keep hacking at me,
      gloating over my errors,
      rejoicing at my failures,
      always looking for the very worst in me?

   I must remember that I truly do belong to God,
   That He does feel for me when I hurt.

   Go ahead, explode, blow up; it doesn't frighten
      God as long as it doesn't hurt anyone else.
   But then, O foolish heart, simmer down,
   And begin renewing your confidence in God.

I hear voices about me whining about the wickedness of the world,
Begging for some divine demonstration of might
   and right.
And yet I know that I have discovered more

delight in my relationship to You
Than they have in their abundant possessions
  and pleasures.

And so I can lie down and sleep in peace.
Because of You, I am eternally secure.

Paraphrase on Psalm 6

O God, don't clobber me in disgust
Or chastise me in anger.
But the fact is, I'm falling apart.
I am distraught and confused.
I am in deep trouble.
And I just don't know how long I can take it.

I can only beg You to enter into my conflict,
To extricate me from its incessant battering,
To demonstrate Your love in deliverance and
  salvation.
Otherwise I'm going down the drain;
And how, then, could I either praise or serve You?

I am fed up with this continual agony;
I can no longer endure these perpetual defeats.
I am becoming increasingly discouraged over my
  human frailties and fallibilities.

If only I could be sure that You know of my
  anguish,
That You discern my cries for help,
That You also feel and understand,
That You will never let me go,

Then I could stand firm even in defeat
And rise victorious even over my failures
And make even my human weaknesses serve
You.

Paraphrase on Psalm 7

O God, I come running to You like a frightened
child.
My pursuers, like hideous monsters, seek to
tear me limb from limb.

O Lord, if I really am to blame for their
hostilities,
If I have willfully hurt anybody,
If I have selfishly blighted another man's
soul,
Then let the ax fall;
I have no right to live; I almost wish I could die.

O God, have mercy.
You know the secrets of my heart and the desires
of my flesh.
You know that I really want so much to do Your
will.
You know my greatest enemy is myself and how
ineffectual I am in dealing with my inner
conflicts.
You know and You have assured me that You care.
You have judged my wickedness;
Now rise up to deliver me from its ugly con-
sequences.

Oh, when will there be an end to evil?
When will this frustrating struggle cease?
I claw like a wounded animal at the promises
    of God for comfort,
I appeal to His love for solace and strength.

I know the end of those who do not repent of
    their sins.
Their selfishness boomerangs; sin kicks back.
They stew in their own juice;
They cut their own throats.

Thus I must persist in running to God in my
    defeats
That I may learn to walk with Him in His
    victories.
I will continue to sing His praises
And to lay claim to His righteousness.

Paraphrase on Psalm 9

My heart overflows with gratitude to God.
I feel so exuberant that I simply must express or
    explode.
I will give voice to my exultations;
I will sing Your praises, O my God.

You helped me to stand firm in spite of those
    who had it in for me,
And they were not successful in their efforts to
    discredit me.

You have destroyed great forces in history that
   rose up to oppose You.
You continue to rule over our fractured world
And sit in judgment over its nations and peoples.
You offer Your strong hand to those who are
   oppressed,
Your loving concern to those who are troubled.
You never hide from those who seek You
Or forsake those who cling to You.

   Sing the praises of God;
   Proclaim loudly His deeds to the people.
   For while He judges evildoers,
   He hears and remembers the cries of those in
      distress.

I need always Your gracious love.
You know all about my inner fears and doubts.
You hold me back from the brink of destruction.
You make it possible for me to sing Your praises
And to rejoice in Your perpetual deliverance.
Ungodly nations sink in their own sewage.
Men who promote evil snare themselves in their
   own nets,
But those who recognize their need of You shall
   be found by You.

Is it any wonder that my heart overflows with
   gratitude to God?

Paraphrase on Psalm 10

Where in the world are You, O God?
Why do You run away when things go wrong?

The sensualist lives by the desires of the flesh.
The materialist seeks for temporal security alone.
The ungodly man indulges in self-worship;
He assumes that "God is dead."

The point is, these are the ones who seem to
  prosper.
They laugh in scorn at those who are inclined
  toward piety.
They claim that they are in the driver's seat and
  cannot be dethroned.
They live and speak arrogantly and carelessly.
They are not concerned about the enslaved and
  the deprived.
They will take what they want irrespective of
  the hurt they cause others.

Wake up, O God! Come out of hiding!
How can You allow these God-defiers to get away
  with it?

O God, You do take note of those in conflict.
You will take account of the godless and the
  arrogant.
You are still Lord over all the world.
You do hear the cries of those who love You;

You are perpetually concerned about their needs.
You will enable them to stand up against the
oppression and pain of this life.

Paraphrase on Psalm 12

O God, help me.
The world is truly going to the dogs.
There is infidelity and deceit on all sides of me.
Every man seems to wear two faces.

And men even boast about their deeds of evil.
They assume that they can talk themselves out
of any corner.
They defy authority and live for themselves alone.

Our God will not forever remain silent.
His voice like thunder will drown out the foolish
boasts of His unfaithful creatures.
"The maligned and the deprived have suffered
long enough," He will say.
"I will rise to their defense and will grant them
My protection."
And what God promises, He will do.

Keep us, great God, from the vile compromises
and the rank complacency of this generation.

Paraphrase on Psalm 20

O my very dear friend,
How much I want to bear your burden, to share
   your trouble!
But I can only pray that God may be very close
   to you in your sorrow
And keep you and protect you in the midst of
   your conflict.
May He remember that you are His own,
That you have dedicated your life to Him,
That your heart's desire is to serve and please
   Him.
May He reach out to touch you and heal you.
May He fulfill your crying need in this hour.
And may we soon rejoice together over your
   deliverance
And walk together in His service.

I know that God does stand by His own,
That our failures do not stay His loving hand,
That He can transform them into victories.
Men about us will put their trust in rockets and
   computers;
But such will fail to solve the real problems of
   our lives.
It is only in the name of God
That we who fall can find the grace to rise again.

Hear my prayer on behalf of my friend, O God.
I want to share his defeat;
May I also share in his victory.

Paraphrase on Psalm 25

I am reaching for You again, O God.
From the abyss of defeat, the suffocating shame of
    failure, I seek Your mercy and Your help.
Enable me to see something of Your will for my
    life.
Break through this stifling darkness with some
    direction, some meaning, some purpose for
    my existence.
You are my God; You have promised me salvation.
How long must I wait for Your response?

Have You given me up, O Lord?
Are You remembering the uncountable times I
    have failed You?
Then I am remembering Your steadfast love,
That Your concern is for those who fail and
    fumble,
That You seek to restore those who humbly reach
    out for You.

I know well that those who walk in Your course
    for their lives find contentment and fulfillment.
I have tried to do so, and again I have failed.
I am aware that those who serve You will know
    true security and abundance.
I have sought this only to be snared and in-
    capacitated by my own weaknesses.

O God, have mercy!
I know my guilt is great.

Look upon my emptiness and loneliness;
Consider kindly my afflictions and despair;
Remember the perpetual presence of my human
   weaknesses and instincts;
Regard once more the pernicious and violent
   forces that oppose Your will in my life;
Forgive me my many sins, and restore me to
   Yourself.
Watch over me and hold on to me, O God, lest
   I fall again.

Paraphrase on Psalm 27

With the living and eternal God as my goal and
   my guide there should be no place in my life
   for fear and anxiety.
All the evil in the world is not able to destroy
   Him;
Nor can it destroy that one who is within His
   loving embrace.
The very legions of hell may lay siege to my soul,
   only to be thwarted by a power that is far
   greater.

I have one primary and ultimate desire:
It is to abide within the love and acceptance of
   God.
I know that I am safe within His tender care
   even in the midst of life's conflicts and trials.

Thus I shall stand tall regardless of the enemies
   that threaten and the forces of evil that en-
   danger my soul.

I will counter the subtle voices of temptation
with exclamations of praise to my God.

My God does hear when I cry out to Him.
He does not ignore my needs, nor is He indifferent to my desires.
He will not let me go even if my very own
family should turn against me.
He will sustain me and keep me on course even
amongst the dangers and pitfalls of this life.

It is possible to know and experience the love of
God in this uncertain and tumultuous
existence.
Take courage, step out in faith, in scorn of
consequences.
Let God have His way with you.

Paraphrase on Psalm 28

O God, I am crying for help!
This is not a pious exclamation;
I mean it! I'm desperate!
If You don't listen, I'll go down the drain!

Don't let me float downstream with those who
ignore You.
I know that they shall go over the edge if they
persist in their course of rebelliousness and
indifference.
Reach forth, O God, and snatch me out of this
overpowering current
Lest I shall perish with them.

I thank You, O God.
You have heard my agonizing cry.
I called for You, and You responded.
You are my Hope and my Salvation.
I will sing Your praises forever.

And thus the Lord is the Hope and Salvation of
    all who trust in Him.
Stay close to those who struggle, O God;
Never let them go.

Paraphrase on Psalm 30

In a world where there are people who assume
    You no longer exist,
I am compelled to proclaim Your praises, O God.
I cannot define nor describe You,
But I know by personal experience Your power
    and presence in my life.
There was a time when I screamed, "Good Lord,
    where are You?"
Then You touched my despairing soul with
    healing,
And You delivered me from my private little
    hell.

Thus I shout God's praises
And exhort all who know Him to do the same.
There are times when I feel God's anger,
But I know that His concern and love for me
    is eternal.

And my nights of despair resolved into the
  dawn of new joy.

There was a time when I thought I was secure
  amidst my material accumulations.
However, they gathered like a cloud to blot
  out the face of God,
And I was left empty and unfulfilled.

I finally came to my senses and returned to You,
  O God.
"Lord," I said, "my well-deserved damnation
  would also be a loss to You.
I cannot praise You from the pits of hell
Or proclaim Your loving-kindness out of the grave
  of eternal death.
So have mercy, Lord, and help me out of this
  tangled web."

And You turned my griping into gratitude,
My screams of despair into proclamations of joy.
Now I can explode with praises,
And I will spend eternity in thanksgiving to You.

Paraphrase on Psalm 32

That man who knows the meaning of forgiveness,
Whose past failures no longer plague him,
Who stands blameless and guilt free before God,
That man is rich indeed.

Everytime I attempt to handle my own guilt—

By ignoring it, rationalizing it, or just running
    away from it —
Some unseen power or pressure from the
    depths of my being squeezes my life dry
And leaves me empty and inadequate.

But when I face up with my failures and
    acknowledge them,
When I open my guilt-ridden heart to You,
    O God,
Then I realize the blessed meaning of for-
    giveness.

Thus everyone who claims faith in a loving God
Needs to cling to the concept of God's acceptance
    and concern.
Times of darkness will come;
Life's storms and tempests will continue to rage;
But he shall not be destroyed by these things.

You are, O God, a place of refuge;
You do enable me to face my problems;
You do keep me from being destroyed by them.
Even within the darkness about us
And in the midst of life's turmoil
One can often hear the voice of God:
"Even these things serve a purpose in your life.

Don't sell them short, for they may be steps along
   My path for you.
Stop being stubborn and stupid like some un-
   discerning jackass that has to be driven with
   sticks or whips."

The faithful and the faithless both suffer the
   uncertainties and insecurities of this life,
But the child of God can depend always on the
   the love of his Father.
It is for this reason that there is light even in the
   midst of darkness
And incomprehensible joy in the midst of sorrow,
And we can find a measure of happiness and
   well-being regardless of the circumstances
   that surround us.

Paraphrase on Psalm 34

I feel at times as if I could never cease praising
   God.
Come and rejoice with me over His goodness!

I reached for Him out of my inner conflicts,
   and He was there to give me strength and
   courage.
I wept in utter frustration over my troubles, and
   He was near to help and support me.
What He has done for me He can do for you.
Turn to Him; He will not turn away from you.
His loving presence encompasses those who
   yield to Him.

He is with them even in the midst of their
    troubles and conflicts.
He meets their emptiness with His abundance
    and shores up their weakness with His divine
    power.

Listen to me; I know whereof I speak.
I have learned th' ough experience that this is
    the way to happiness.
God is ever alert to the cries of His children;
He feels and bears with them their pains and
    problems.
He is very near to those who suffer
And reaches out to help those who are battered
    down with despair.

Even the children of God must experience
    affliction,
But they have a loving God who will keep them
    and watch over them.
The godless suffers in loneliness and without
    hope;
The servant of God finds meaning and purpose
    even in the midst of his suffering and conflict.

Paraphrase on Psalm 36

It is amazing to me how some people can be so
    utterly self-centered
And so indifferent and calloused to the desires
    and needs of others.
Not only do they neglect God,

They are totally oblivious of Him and have no
fear of Him.
And then they manage to convince themselves
that this is life,
That the world spins around them,
And they must satiate their own desires irrespective of the hurt it causes others.

And yet Your all-pervading love, O God,
Which extends far beyond the dimensions of
our conscious lives,
Includes even these distorted people who spurn
You in exchange for lives that are twisted and
self-centered.

Your eternal love is beyond comprehension.
It is no wonder that Your children reach inces-
santly for it and find security within it.
Within that love, O Lord,
Is the answer to our needs
And the fulfillment of our desires.

Continue to pour out Your saving love upon those
who follow You.
Do not allow the arrogance and infidelity of the
godless to deter me from Your course for my
life.

Paraphrase on Psalm 38

O God, how angry You must be with me!
I feel as if I were pierced through with a red-hot
    iron of conviction
And stifled with the heavy hand of judgment.

I am falling apart;
I am sick unto death with sin and failure.
I am broken and spent.
I am wretched and miserable.
I am flat on my face in despair.

Even those I once called my friends now keep
    their distance
While others actually gloat over my predicament.
But I am becoming numb even to their glances of
    suspicion or pity and their self-righteous
    rebukes.
I have ceased trying to defend myself
Or responding to their accusations.
I've had it; I am ready to throw in the towel;
I simply cannot take it any longer.

You are aware of my anguish.
You feel something of my misery.
I know that I have grieved You;
And I am truly sorry for my sin.

Don't turn away from me, O God;
Don't leave me in this abominable mess.
Save me now, O God, lest I be damned forever.

Paraphrase on Psalm 39

I said to myself, "I'll watch it—
I'll grit my teeth and hold in my hostilities at
  least as long as I am in the midst of ungodly
  people."

And I honestly tried, but it was no use.
The pressures increased.
The more I stewed about it, the more frustrated
  I became.

Finally I exploded:
"O God, demonstrate some concern for me.
Give me some reason for this incessant conflict,
Some objective for this fast-ebbing life of mine.
You made me what I am—a bubble or a bag of gas,
And the span of my existence is but a speck of
  dust to You.
It is true about every man.
He is no more than a smidgen of moist air
Or a shadow without lasting substance.
Man enters and endures this temporal turmoil for
  no reason whatsoever.
He agonizes and toils only to leave the fruits
  for someone else to enjoy.

"So I wonder what in the world it's all about.
I have no hope at all except in You.
I continue to lay claim to Your forgiveness for my
  failures.
Keep them from making me a despised and

abhorred creature in the sight of men.
Lift Your heavy hand from me;
I am utterly weary of its oppressing weight.
When You punish a man with judgment of his
   failures,
You suck up like a tornado everything that is
   precious to him.
Surely man is no more than a passing cloud on
   the eternal horizon.

"Hear and decipher these confusing thoughts
   of mine;
Lend Your ear to these agonizing cries;
Turn not away from my pains and problems.
I am just a swiftly passing traveler as were all
   men before me.
Turn Your scornful eye away from me.
Let me have just a morsel of happiness before
   I leave this world and enter into oblivion."

Paraphrase on Psalm 40

I searched long and shouted loud for God.
It finally paid off, and He responded.
He reached into my pathetic emptiness and
   planted objective and purpose there.
Now I feel like singing;
There is genuine meaning for my life.
And maybe I can sell others on this concept of
   really finding themselves in God.
Those who are thoroughly fed up with the fly-by-
   night objectives of this ephemeral existence,

Who will look to their Creator and seek out His
     will for them,
They will also find something to sing about.
There is love and concern there,
And meaning and purpose,
Far more than one can possibly imagine,

Our God is not looking for genius;
He does not require great talents.
He is not charmed by our panic-ridden activity.
He simply asks for our faith and our obedience.
It was when I turned from self-seeking to em-
     brace His will for my life
That I discovered serenity and security.

Thus I am compelled to express in word and in
     deed the glad news of God's love and concern
     to anyone who will listen.
And the Lord knows that I have honestly tried
     to do this.
My frailties and my failures are many,
But I have not cheated on this score.
I have proclaimed the salvation that God offers
     to all.

But my conflicts have not ceased.
My sin-permeated nature still plagues me.
I still feel overwhelmed at times by my faults and
     fallibilities.
I am disturbed and depressed when others fail
     to understand or accept me.
I need to rely continuously on the grace of God.

God grant that all who search for life's meaning
     may discover such in a relationship of love and
     trust in Him.

They shall then know His greatness and proclaim
  His praises.
As for me, foolish and sinful though I am,
I know that God will never cease to love me.

Paraphrase on Psalm 42

As a desert wanderer longs for springs of cool
  water,
So my thirsty soul reaches out for You, O God.
How I long for a deeper sense of Your presence,
For a faith that will embrace You without fear
  or doubt!
Yet while I weep in longing,
People about me say, "If God is not dead, where
  is He?"

I remember so well the faith of my childhood.
How real God was to me in those days when I
  prayed and sang praises and listened to His
  Word in the fellowship of family and friends!
Then why am I so depressed now?
Why cannot I recapture the joy and confidence of
  those years?
I remember the stories of Your love that I had
  been taught;
How merciful and all-powerful were Your
  dealings with Your children throughout history!
Yet now my heart is empty,
And waves of doubt flood over my soul.

I pray; but the heavens, too, are empty.

It is almost as if God had forgotten all about me.
And while I struggle with the sickness of doubt,
People about me say, "If God is not dead, where is He?"

O foolish heart, why do you seethe in unrest?
God has not changed; His love for me is ever the same.
I must renew my faith in God;
I must again shout His praises even when I don't feel His presence.
For truly He is God, and He is my Help and my Hope.

Paraphrase on Psalm 46

Our great God is still our Refuge and Strength;
He is ever aware of our problems and concerned about our fears.
Thus we have no business doubting Him, even though the earth is convulsed in tragedy or its human masses are threatened by nuclear annihilation.

God continues to reign as all-wise and as almighty as ever.
His eternal plan is not canceled out by the whims of men or the freakish accidents of nature.
Nations will destroy each other;
Civilizations will perish;
The earth itself may one day become a smoking cinder,

But God will not leave us.
He is forever our sure Refuge and Strength.

Just look about you; read the pages of history.
Refresh your flagging spirits with the reminder of
    His great feats throughout the ages.
And you will again hear Him speaking:
"Relax, stop fretting, and remember that I am
    still Your God;
And I still hold the reins on this world of yours."

God is here amongst us;
He continues to be our Refuge and Strength.

Paraphrase on Psalm 53

Those who proclaim that God is dead are
    veritable fools.
They presume to speak as sophisticated
    intellectuals;
They are in reality, even unconsciously,
    promoting depravity.

God is ever probing the hearts of men,
Marking those who are wise enough to seek after
    Him.

He finds instead that the great masses of His
    creatures are following after other gods.
And without realizing it,
They are leading one another into certain
    destruction.

It is no wonder there is such confusion and terror
in the world about us.
It is for most part perpetuated by those who have
no use for God.
Oh, may our great God restore the hearts of men
to Himself!

Paraphrase on Psalm 57

Encompass me with Your love and mercy,
gracious Lord;
I have no security except in You.
I am perpetually exposed to the destructive
forces of this existence.
I am in constant danger of losing the battle to
the very passions and desires of my own nature.
I can only submit myself to You
And believe that You will fulfill Your purposes
in me.

Your love, O God, is steadfast;
Your grace is everlasting.

Even when I am beaten down by depression
And ensnared by my weaknesses and frailties
And my own lust threatens to devour me,
You are my God, and You will not let me go.

I am determined to serve You, O Lord.
May my life be a continual thankoffering to You.
I shall sing Your praises forever.

Paraphrase on Psalm 61

Listen to me, O God;
Listen to what I have to say.
From the bowels of this fractured world I cry
out my fears and my longings.

I cannot find peace or security
Until I lose myself in something or someone
that is greater than I.
Draw me more deeply into Your life and
purposes;
Only then will I find shelter from the tempests
of this fearful and uncertain existence.

You know that I am committed to You.
And as I am so committed, I have inherited the
same divine promises that are given to all who
follow You.
Grant to me the grace to fulfill my pledge of
loyalty and service,
And I shall never cease to sing Your praises.

Paraphrase on Psalm 62

As for me, my heart waits on God.
I know that my salvation comes from Him.
I may change my views about many things;
But in respect to my need for God and His love,
  that is one conviction which shall never
  change.

There are many who would like to sabotage a
  man's deepest convictions.
With the skillful use of words and logic they try
  to destroy the very foundations of his faith.
As for me, my heart waits on God.
He is my Hope and my Help.
The temporal values that men focus on are so
  quickly lost amidst the tempests of this life.
Their highest aspirations burst forth like bright
  flares, only to fizzle out like wet fuses.

But my God offers a security that is eternal.
It cannot be logically defined, but it can be
  experienced.
Commit your life to Him,
And you shall discover an anchor that will hold
  firm despite the chaos of this existence or the
  prattle of godless intellectuals.

Paraphrase on Psalm 63

Like a thirsty child reaching for a drink,
I grasp for You, O God.
And I have found You.
I have sensed Your holy presence in the worship
    service;
And in the hour of prayer I have felt You to be
    near.
I realize now that Your love for me is far better
    than life itself.

My heart is full of joy and contentment.
My mouth is filled with praises for You.
Even the night hours are no longer lonely
As I contemplate Your tender concern for me.

The enemies of my soul still seek to betray me,
But they shall not snatch me out of Your hand.
And now that I have found You,
I shall be secure and happy forever.

Paraphrase on Psalm 64

Listen to me, O God;
I think I have good reason to complain.

I try very hard to follow in Your paths and to
serve in Your purposes.
But I am so deeply disturbed over the enemies
and pitfalls that I unsuspectingly meet around
every corner.
I find them in the tumultuous passions of my own
being.
Much as I seek to rid myself of these over-
whelming forces,
They continue to clutch at my soul and to trip
me up as I strive to please You.
I become so tired of this perpetual conflict with
my sin-permeated nature.
And then I run into the opposition in the reactions
of well-trusted friends.
Their suspicions and unjust criticisms leave me
withered and dried up in depression and
discouragement.
And now it is the cunning words of the worldly-
wise, even the intellectual giants of this age,
that threaten the very foundations of what I
so intensely believed in.

I must renew my faith and continue to believe
that those who foolishly oppose You will fail
in their attempts to thwart Your purposes
And that those who trust in You are truly and
eternally secure even in the midst of this
conflict and antagonism that swirls incessantly
about them.

Paraphrase on Psalm 65

You well deserve the praises of men, O God;
And they should fulfill their pledges to You.

Everyone must eventually face up with You,
And it must be with all of his sins and short-
    comings.
But that one who comes in sorrow and repentance
    shall find You merciful and gracious.
You shall forgive his sins,
And You shall reconcile him to Your kingdom and
    shall fill his heart with Your love and joy.

O God, You reach out to save us,
You are the single, eternal Hope of all mankind.

You make Your power known to us in the majestic
    grandeur of the mountains
And in the thunderous roar of the ocean's waves.
Your abundance is poured out upon us in the
    grain-laden fields, the flocks in the meadows,
    the gentle rain that caresses the green hills.
Your love for us is manifested in Your great acts
    of deliverance on our behalf.

You well deserve the praises of men, O God.

Paraphrase on Psalm 66

It is high time we start making happy noises about God,
That we boldly proclaim His name and shout His praises.

We already know what He has done throughout history, the great deeds He performed, the people who witnessed them and worshiped Him.
Let us recognize, as well, what He is constantly doing for us.

He draws us into the crucible of conflict;
He tests and tries us in the valley of pain and sorrow;
He allows us to taste the agony of affliction;
He gives our enemies permission to oppose and oppress us.
And then He uses these very things to purge and prepare us for His purposes.

Now I renew my pledge to my God.
I strive to carry out those promises I made to Him when I cried for His help in my troubles.
I yield up to Him my life as a sacrifice and thank-offering.

You who are seeking for God,
These are the things that He has done for me:

He has accepted me despite my sins and failures.
He does listen when I cry out to Him,
And He responds with solace and support.

I proclaim God's praises because I know that
He will love me forever.

Paraphrase on Psalm 67

May we continually be the recipients of God's
mercy and blessing
In order that we may demonstrate His order and
purpose throughout the earth
And His redemptive power to the creatures of
this world.

And may it ultimately resolve in all of God's sons
Lifting their voices in praise to their Lord and
God.

The nations of the earth would truly abide in
peace and sing for joy
If they would allow God to be their God
And if they would direct their destinies according
to His will.

Then the inhabitants of this world would surely
lift their voices in praise to their Lord and God.

The earth continues to receive the abundance
of God.
His blessings are all about us.

May every mountain and valley, plain and forest,
May every city street with its teeming apartments
 and sprawling suburbs
Echo with the praises of men to their God.

Paraphrase on Psalm 69

O God, this time I am really up against the wall;
I'm at the bottom of the barrel, the end of my
 rope.
There is no place to go but up.
Save me, O God, before it is too late.

I can't even cry out any longer;
I can't even pray, so deep is my despair.

O Lord, You know the ugliness of my failure.
How sorely it must grieve You!
Forbid that others may be hurt by my foolishness,
That my errors and faults might lead them astray.
I have been trying to represent You before them;
Instead I have brought dishonor and disrespect
 on my witness and Your name.
Now even those who once loved me keep their
 distance;
And those who listened in respect turn away in
 disgust.

Maybe it has been my intense eagerness to carry
 out Your purposes that has become my stum-
 bling block.
And now I am being ridiculed for my zeal.

They make fun of me; they whisper about me
   behind my back.

O God, don't let me go down the drain.
Respond, in Your great love, to my unhappy
   plight.
Raise me from the mire of despair, the darkness
   of depression.
Deliver me from these human weaknesses that
   beset me and lead me into defeat.
You know what they are, O Lord.
And You know the limits of my endurance.
You know, as well, the pain of my failure and the
   abject loneliness that one feels when he loses
   the battle.

You know, O God, and You reach forth in mercy
   to rescue and deliver.
You sometimes permit failure and defeat in my
   life, only to revive and renew my relationship
   to You.
Thus I will again sing the praises of God.
And make thankofferings to Him.

May all those who are beaten down by failure and
   despair see anew Your love and experience
   Your deliverance and be restored to joy and
   purposefulness once more.

Paraphrase on Psalm 70

O God, may You take pleasure in setting me free
    and in securing me from the enemies of my
    soul.
Keep them from bringing shame upon Your
    servant and dishonor upon Your name.

May those who sincerely seek You find genuine
    happiness and fulfillment.
And may they express their joy in proclamations
    of praise to God.
As for me, I am always in need of Your sustaining
    grace.
O God, do not withhold it from me.

Paraphrase on Psalm 71

Good Lord, You have kept me within the secure
    embrace of Your love these many years.
My life is one long list of divine deliverances.
I have come running to You again and again
    when the forces of evil set themselves against
    me.

From the moment of my birth I was dedicated

to Your will, given life by You, only to yield
it back to You.
And since that time the days and hours of my
life have been filled with praise for You.
But the enemies that plagued me in my youth
still lay siege to my soul, looking for chinks in
my armor, for loopholes in my defenses through
which to enter and lay waste.

Now, as I near the late afternoon and evening
of my life,
I continue to seek out Your love and mercy.
Even while I shout Your praises and proclaim
Your salvation,
I reach for the assurance of Your love and con-
cern.

You have guided me through my precarious
youth,
Now I need Your grace for my senior years.
Fill my heart with purpose and my mouth with
praises
That I may continue to proclaim Your name and
Your salvation to all who will listen.

You are, O God, the Creator and Performer of
great and glorious things.
There is no one like You.
You have kept me amidst life's conflicts,
Led me through its crucible of experiences,
And drawn me back from its pitfalls and preci-
pices,
And You have healed my wounds and comforted
me amidst my afflictions.
Thus I know that You will continue to love and
care for me.

I will dedicate my remaining days to praising
You,
Espousing Your faithfulness and proclaiming
Your love and concern for all who will turn
to You.
May every fiber of my being and every activity
of my life resound with praises to my God.

Paraphrase on Psalm 73

It is generally expected that God will stand by
the righteous
And relate to those whose deeds and thoughts
are purely altruistic.
I am afraid I just don't belong to that class of
people.
I guess I am just a perpetual backslider.
Rather than thinking unselfishly,
I find myself envious and covetous about those
who have so much more than I.

They never seem to have problems.
They are always so strong and healthy.
I doubt that they know the meaning of conflict.
They are proud, carefree, devil-may-care, even
malicious, and so disgustingly smug about
it all.
They act as if God didn't even exist,
And they are almost blasphemous in their atti-
tudes and actions.

And yet people will honor and applaud them;

They find nothing to censor about them.
What aggravates me is their obvious unconcern
  about God or fellowman.
Yet they always appear to be so comfortable and
  well off.
And all the while I struggle so desperately with
  my sin-permeated nature.
I try so hard to please God.
Yet my days are full of conflict,
And my heart seethes in unrest.

I know I speak foolishly and unfairly,
But I get so fed up with it all.
That is, until I begin arguing with God about it.
Then I realize that they are not as well off as they
  appear to be.
Their bright bubble will burst one day;
Their dream will turn into a nightmare.

It's just that I get so depressed at times,
And I act like a stupid fool.
What is so amazing is that even amidst these
  irrational and unspiritual contemplations
I am never far from You.
You hold me close to Yourself.
You guide me and watch over me.
You assure me that it is all worth it.
And because of this glorious truth
I really have no need for anything else.
The essential desires of my being are met in You.
I shall often be victimized by human failure,
But my great God never ceases to love me and
  bless me.

How good it is to know that God is always near!

Paraphrase on Psalm 77

I cry to God in my desperation.
Out of the dark corner of my stifling loneliness
I grope in vain for some solace or comfort.

I try to think about God,
To contemplate His many promises;
But my heart is empty,
My soul as dry as dust.
I spend sleepless nights searching,
Waiting for God to speak to my need, to give me
    strength in my conflict.
I remember how He has responded to my prayers
    in times past.
But I get nothing from Him now,
Nothing save the echoes of my own agonies as
    they are screamed into empty heavens.

I am reminded of His deeds and wonders of
    years past.
He demonstrated His love in His concern for His
    people.
His majesty and power is reflected in the great
    forces of nature about me.
Then why doesn't He hear my pitiful pleadings?
Why doesn't He fulfill His promises on my
    behalf?
Good Lord, where are You?

Paraphrase on Psalm 84

O God, the center of Your will is truly the place
of fulfillment.
I long incessantly for the peace and security of
walking with You.
Therein only is purpose and meaning for my life.

Even the birds of the air and the animals that
inhabit our forests
Abide within Your orbit and destiny for them.
Thus it is that the man who discovers and follows
Your course for him is forever blessed.

How enriched they are who draw their power
from You, whose hearts are focused on You!
Even as they wend their way through this fractured world,
They become springs of healing, reservoirs of
power, to the sick, weak, and empty lives they
touch about them.

O Lord, look with loving mercy upon those who
have yielded their destinies to You.
Just one day in the center of Your will is incom-
parably better than a thousand days spent in
the pursuit of self-centered aims and objectives.
It is more fulfilling to be an underpaid clerk in
the service of my God
Than to be the owner and director of some huge
and wealthy enterprise.

O God, nothing that is truly good and worth-
while is withheld from those who walk within
Your will.
The man who trusts in You is very rich indeed.

Paraphrase on Psalm 86

O Lord, my prayer to You is always out of a life
that is full of need.
I am Your servant; I am trying to represent You.
I need Your support for every step I take.
How gracious You are to hear my plea
and respond to my cry
and pour out Your forgiving love upon me!

Men are so foolish in the things they love and
worship.
You alone are God,
And You alone possess the healing grace that
can succor and sustain their fickle hearts.
Continue to lead me in Your course for my life.
Enable me to walk in the way of truth.
Draw together in loving obedience to You all
the members and senses of my body and being.
Then I shall glorify You forever, and my life
shall be a perpetual thankoffering to You.

I find the daily journey difficult and painful.
There are forces within me and about me that
are much too strong for me.
But You are a loving and patient God.
Continue to have mercy upon me,
to deliver me from my selfish involvements,

to forgive me my sins and failures,
to shore up the weak places in my life.
Help me to feel something of Your loving acceptance and to reflect to others the joy of being
Your son and servant.

Paraphrase on Psalm 88

O God, I need You every day that I exist
and every night that I pass through.
Never turn Your face from me, O Lord,
for my life is a perpetual plea for help.

My life is one long series of conflicts and defeats,
And they only increase as I near its end.
My ultimate destiny is a hole in the ground,
but even now I am as good as dead.
Without strength, forsaken, shunned by my
fellowmen,
I feel as if I were separated forever from You.
I am assailed by afflictions,
beset by obsessions,
and all but forgotten by God and man.

And yet I continue to cry out to You.
Even while the assaults of this life
and the fear of death
surround me and close in on me,
I look to You for some ray of hope.

Good Lord, where are You?
Is there nothing within me worth saving?

Paraphrase on Psalm 90

O God, You have always been God.
Long before the earth was formed,
Long after it ceases to exist,
You have been and You shall always be.

With You there is no beginning or end;
Time is not measured by decades or centuries.
Our precious lives, so important to us, are but
  fleeting shadows to You.
And they are so full of trouble and conflict and
  so marked by sin and failure.

O God, break into our short span of existence
  with Your eternal love and grace.
May our days of despair be interspersed with
  hours of joy.
Enable us to see something of Your will and
  purpose for our creation and to discover some
  meaning for our brief and trouble-fraught
  appearance in this world.
Imprint upon us Your brand of ownership, and
  place us within Your plan and objective for
  our lives.

Paraphrase on Psalm 91

That one whose faith is focused on God,
Who finds his security in Him,
Does not have to live in fear.
He is not left untouched by the tempests of this
life,
And he may be wounded by the onslaughts of
evil,
But his great God does not leave him to suffer
these things alone.
The Lord cares for His own and delivers him
even in the midst of the conflicts that plague
him.

If God is truly your God,
You do not have to be afraid of the enemy that
threatens or the affliction that lays you low.
Men all about you may fall, never to rise again,
But the Lord is by your side to raise you to your
feet and to lead you to ultimate victory.

Even the ministering spirits of His invisible
world are watching over you.
They will not allow anything to hurt you except
by God's loving permission and through His
eternal concern.

Our loving God has promised it:
"Because My child loves Me, I will never let
him go.

I shall feel the pain of his wounds and bear his
    hurt and shall transform that which is ugly
    into that which enriches and blesses.
And when he cries out in agony, I shall hear
    and answer him.
I will be close to him and will deliver him,
    and I will grant him eternal life."

Paraphrase on Psalm 100

Break forth into exclamations of joy and glad-
    ness,
    you who serve the Lord!

God is not dead! He is ever our God!
He made us; we belong to Him;
We are His sons and servants.
And His love for us never runs out;
His care and concern for us will go on forever.

Let the world see our manifestations of joy!
Let us lift up our voices in songs of praise
And surrender our lives as perpetual offerings
    of thanksgiving!
Let us bless His name forever!

Paraphrase on Psalm 102

Good Lord, where are You?
If You really do exist,
Why don't You come out of hiding
And do something about this creature in distress?

I am physically weary;
I am mentally depressed;
I am spiritually defeated.
I can't eat; I can't sleep.
I am like garbage, discarded refuse in the back
    alley;
Like yesterday's newspaper shuffled around by
    the wind.
I feel like some sort of zombi,
Some nonentity, some nothing that people, if
    they acknowledge, would only curse.
I eat crow and drink gall.
Now even You have tossed me aside like some
    moth-eaten garment that no one could possibly
    want.

But the prophets have proclaimed Your name,
And the Scriptures declare Your mercy,
And the old saints pass on Your promises.
You do reign over our world, they say,
You do show concern for the poor clods of this
    earth.

Good Lord, prove it!

Look down from wherever You are on Your
creatures who are wallowing in wretchedness.
Deliver us, O God, set us free!

I must take comfort in Your everlastingness;
That You who outlive the seasons and the cen-
turies,
Who have blessed the saints of the past,
Can also care for Your servants in this fearful
hour.
For Your years have no end,
Nor do the destinies of those who trust in You.

Paraphrase on Psalm 103

My heart is bursting with praises to God;
Every fiber of my being reaches out in rejoicing!
How can I ever forget His many blessings?
    He forgives all my sins;
    He touches my afflictions with healing;
    He snatches me back from the gaping jaws of
      hell;
    He covers me with concern and love;
    He fulfills my deepest desires and gives me
      meaning for life and purpose for living.

God is a God of justice and judgment,
But He is on the side of those who need His help.
He is angry with those who persistently rebel
against Him,
But He pours out His love upon those who turn
to Him.

He does not give us our just deserts
Or pay us what we well deserve.
He is grieved when we so miserably fail,
But He quickly draws us to His forgiving heart
    and accepts us just as if it never happened.
He looks with tenderness upon His faltering
    children;
He knows and understands our fallible natures.

Man by himself is a pitiful picture of weakness.
Now and then one will, like a streaking meteor,
    blaze out across the skies of time,
Only to become a smoking cinder at the end of
    his short journey.
But those who tie on to God's loving will and
    purposes
Become the objects of His eternal mercy and
    righteousness.

Rejoice with me, you who are His invisible
    servants
And you who hear and obey His voice.
Shout His praises, you who are His children
And you who serve as His ministers and priests.
There is no time for despair and discouragement.
Whoever and wherever you are, lift your hearts
    in praises to God.

Paraphrase on Psalm 107

Those who have experienced the redemption of
  God and know what it means to be reconciled
  to Him
Ought to dedicate their very lives to serving Him
And their voices to proclaiming to the world
  His loving grace.

Some of you have known the meaning of emptiness and loneliness.
You have drunk from many wells and sipped
  honey from many flowers and stumbled into
  many blind alleys in your search for fulfillment.
But your hearts remained empty and unsatisfied.
Then you faced up with God and His claim on
  You, and you discovered purpose and objective
  for your lives.
Don't keep it to yourselves! Tell it to the world!
Proclaim in word and deed the wonderful works
  of a loving God.
Let others know that He is able to fill their emptiness and satiate their hunger.

Some of you have endured long nights of suffocating darkness.
You know well the dregs of depression, the power
  of obsession, the clutch of despair and frustration on your souls.
You fell on your faces in defeat, and no one
  seemed to care.

Then in desperation you cried out to God in your
    misery;
And He flooded your lives with light and hope.
Thank God! It is by His eternal love that you
    are delivered.
Tell others about His power to deliver them
    from that which binds them or blinds them.

Some of you have followed sin's cruel conse-
    quences into the crucible of sickness and pain.
You were led to the very brink of destruction.
Then you turned to God in the midst of your
    great distress,
And He touched you with His healing and deliv-
    ered you from your afflictions.
Rejoice in God! Let your praises ascend to Him!
Proclaim His healing grace to others who may
    be ready to listen.

Some of you have set out in joyous abandon to
    find your happiness in the streets and market-
    places of the great city.
But you became lost and disillusioned and afraid.
The exciting city became a devouring monster
    that threatened to dehumanize and destroy you.
You cried out for help, and you found that God
    was there amongst its milling masses.
He restored courage to your hearts and meaning
    to your lives.
You discovered purpose and validity and sig-
    nificance in the loving acceptance of your God.
Let the city's multitudes hear about your dis-
    covery!
Let them know that God is near that they may
    rejoice in His everlasting and ever-present
    love.

It is the lack of God in a person's life that dries him up and turns him into dust.

It is God's presence and acceptance that turns on the lights and floods the dark corridors that lead nowhere and transforms them into warm rooms wherein one may live in joy and fulfillment.

It is the acknowledgment of a loving God that makes the forbidding city a place to live in and its God-fearing inhabitants glowing reflections of His eternal concern.

Great God, be it city street or mountaintop,
May it become my pulpit from which to proclaim Your praises,
And my workbench from which to transmit Your love to the lives of lonely men.

Paraphrase on Psalm 121

Where should I look for help in my need?
To the majestic mountain peaks that probe our skies
Or the giants of industry that hem in our cities?
To the satellites that circle our world
Or the computers that store up our knowledge?

The answer to my problems, the fulfillment of my needs must come from God Himself,
From Him who created the skies and the mountains and man to dwell in their midst.

He is a great God who knows our every desire,
Whose watchful eye is upon us night and day.
We can make no move without His knowledge.
His concern for His children is constant;
His love for them is eternal.

And thus the Lord will keep you,
Shielding you from the forces of evil as a shade
  tree shields you from the rays of the blazing
  sun.

He does care for you,
And He will fight with you against the enemies
  of your soul.
Whether you be coming or going,
He knows the course you take;
And He will go before you.

Paraphrase on Psalm 130

O God, tonight I seek for You out of a heart full
  of guilt and a mind full of bewilderment and
  frustration.
You have heard me before and responded with
  grace and mercy.
Now I seek You again.

I know I am guilty, O God;
But if You kept account of man's failings and
  fallings, no one could ever face You again.
I reach for You because You look with loving
  mercy upon my wretched soul.

You will accept me and forgive me and reinstate
    me in Your purposes.

It is no wonder that I return again and again to
    God.
I long for His forgiveness and acceptance more
    than the night watchman longs for the dawn
    of day.

Thus I plead with you to focus your faith on God.
You will find love there—and salvation.
And He will cleanse you of your sin
And restore you to His loving heart.

Paraphrase on Psalm 131

O God, I have failed because I expected too much
    of myself.
I have fallen because I focused too much on
    success and have reckoned too little with my
    own humanity.

It is time that I still my restless heart and quiet
    my overambitious spirit.

It is far better that we center our aspirations on
    God and His will for our lives.

Paraphrase on Psalms 133 and 134

O God, how precious it is for us
And how pleasing it must be to You
When Your sons and servants learn how to live
    and work together in unity!

It is in the measure that we do this that we begin
    to resemble You
And to carry out most effectively Your purposes
    in our disjointed and discordant world.

Come, let us together bless His name,
    rejoice in His loving concern for us,
    declare His worth to all creatures,
    and walk in obedience to His will.

It is the same God who made heaven and earth
    and all of us who dwell therein.
Let us worship and serve Him together.

Paraphrase on Psalm 138

I am exceedingly grateful, O Lord,
For You have heard my cries and complaints,
And You responded with mercy and strength.
Now my life is overflowing with thanksgiving,

And my mouth is filled with Your praises.

If only the leaders of our disjointed world would
    listen to Your words and direct their people in
    accordance with Your will,
They would then know the meaning of peace,
And they would rejoice in the ways of God.

You have not shielded me from the pains of
    trouble or the ravages of conflict,
But You have kept me even in the midst of
    sorrow and suffering.
You take my side against the enemies of my soul,
And You will not allow them to destroy me.

Thus I know You will fulfill Your purpose for my
    life.
Your love and mercy is everlasting;
You will not let me go.

Paraphrase on Psalm 139

O God, You know me inside and out, through and
    through.
Everything I do,
    every thought that flits through my mind,
    every step I take,
    every plan I make,
    every word I speak,
You know, even before these things happen.
You know my past;
You know my future.

Your circumventing presence covers my every
move.
Your knowledge of me sometimes comforts me,
sometimes frightens me;
But always it is far beyond my comprehension.

There is no way to escape You, no place to hide.
If I ascend to the heights of joy,
You are there before me.
If I am plunged into the depths of despair,
You are there to meet me.
I could fly to the other side of our world
and find You there to lead the way.
I could walk into the darkest of nights,
only to find You there to lighten its dismal
hours.

You were present at my very conception.
You guided the development of my unformed
members within the body of my mother.
Nothing about me, from beginning to end, was
hid from Your eyes.
How frightfully and fantastically wonderful it
all is!

May Your all-knowing, everywhere-present
Spirit continue to search out my feelings and
thoughts.
Deliver me from that which may hurt or destroy
me,
And guide me along the paths of love and truth.

Paraphrase on Psalm 142

I direct my cries to the Lord.
Out of the ear-piercing sounds
  and the ceaseless turmoil
  of this concrete jungle
  I speak God's name.
For my heart is deeply troubled and depressed,
  and I feel weary and faint.

I am confused and lost.
I cannot find my way.
The nameless faces that flit by take no notice
  of me.
No one knows my name,
And no one cares.

I turn to You, O God.
You have heard me before,
And You responded to my cries.
Perhaps even amidst the frustrating activity and
  the crowded streets of the great city
You can hear the cries of a lonely child.

O God, deliver me from my prison of loneliness.
Turn my cries of distress into proclamations
  of joy.
Direct my steps into the fellowship of others
  who love and serve You.

Paraphrase on Psalm 146

Praise God!
As long as I have breath in my body,
I will praise God!

Don't pin your hopes on the genius of man.
His ultimate end is the same as yours,
And he becomes once more like the dust from
  which he came.

That person is secure who draws his strength
  from God.
He who created the earth and all that abides
  on it,
He is that One who can heal the wounds and
  mend the fractures of this disjointed world.
He can break the bonds of obsession
And pierce man's stupor with visions of truth.
He tenderly reaches out to those who are
  oppressed
And reveals His concern for those who are lost
  and lonely.
He watches over His own
While the paths of the godless lead to their own
  destruction.

This is the God who cannot die!
Praise God!
Amen!